INTRODUCT

Introduction: Infidelity: 21 Reasons Men Cheat: A Guide for Women Seeking a Lasting, Fulfilling Relationship

Infidelity is a topic that has left many individuals feeling hurt, confused, and searching for answers. When broken trust can shake the foundation of a relationship, leaving behind a wake of emotional turmoil. This eBook is not about casting blame but rather understanding why cheating occurs and how you, as a partner, can take informed steps to build a more resilient, satisfying relationship.

In "Infidelity: 21 Reasons Men Cheat," we'll explore some of the most common reasons men stray, helping you gain insight into the psychological, emotional, and situational factors that can play a role. Understanding these patterns and behaviors can better protect your relationship from these pitfalls. This guide will empower you with tools for self-awareness, communication, and emotional strength—tools that can help create a lasting and fulfilling partnership.

This isn't about control or placing the full responsibility of a relationship on your shoulders. Rather, it's about learning how to foster a connection that both partners value deeply. Through practical advice, real-world insights, and a compassionate approach, this book aims to give you clarity and strategies that help nurture trust and intimacy in your relationship. Whether single, dating, or married, these insights can help you build and maintain the relationship you deserve.

Let's dive in together, uncovering each layer to help you better understand the complexities of commitment, attraction, and trust, ultimately empowering you to create a stronger, more enduring connection with your partner.

Chapter 1

Lack of Emotional Connection

Men, like women, need emotional intimacy. If a man feels emotionally disconnected from his partner, he may seek solace in someone who provides the emotional support and validation he craves. This could be a lack of communication or feeling misunderstood in the relationship.

To maintain a strong emotional bond in a long-term marriage or relationship, here's my advice based on experience:

Openly and Often Communicate

Open communication is the foundation of an emotional bond. Make it a habit to share your thoughts, feelings, and experiences about your day, dreams, or challenges; be open and honest; and encourage your partner to do the same. This creates a safe space where both of you feel heard and understood.

Express Appreciation

Never underestimate the power of showing gratitude and appreciation. Acknowledge the little things your partner does and express how much they mean to you. It makes the other person feel valued and loved, deepening your connection.

Stay Curious About Each Other

After many years, it's easy to assume you know everything about your partner. However, people change and evolve. Stay curious about each other's interests, goals, and dreams.   Ask questions that dive deeper into their feelings and desires, keeping the relationship dynamic and fresh.

Prioritize Quality Time Together

It's essential to carve out time for the two of you away from distractions. Whether it's a nights walks together, or quiet moments in the evening or making time to connect emotionally. These moments help strengthen your bond and create shared experiences.

Offer Emotional Support

Life comes with ups and downs, and being there for your partner emotionally is crucial. Listen when they need to talk, comfort them during tough times, and celebrate their victories. Knowing that you have each other's back builds a deep sense of trust and closeness.

Keep Physical Intimacy Alive

Emotional intimacy and physical connection often go hand in hand. Even simple gestures like holding hands, hugging, or kissing throughout the day can nurture an emotional bond and maintain closeness.

In short, it's about staying connected, being present, and showing love in small, meaningful ways.

CHAPTER 2

Boredom and Routine

Long-term relationships can sometimes fall into routines that lead to boredom. Men may cheat when they seek excitement or the thrill of something new, feeling trapped in monotony and craving a spark they believe is missing from their current relationship.

To keep boredom and routine from creeping into a long-term marriage or relationship, here's my advice from experience:

Keep Things Spontaneous and Exciting

Routine can be a relationship killer if left unchecked, so breaking out of the habits is key. Here's how to keep the spark alive:

Surprise Each Other

Surprises don't have to be grand gestures—simple, thoughtful actions can keep the excitement alive. Plan a spontaneous date night, leave a sweet note, or cook their favorite meal unexpectedly. Small surprises show you're still invested in making them happy and keeping things fresh.

Try New Experiences Together

Shared experiences help build memories and excitement. Try a new hobby, explore a new place, or learn something new together. Whether it's traveling to a new destination, taking a cooking class, or doing something adventurous, new activities can reignite the fun and sense of discovery in your relationship.

Revisit the Past

Reliving special moments from the early days of your relationship can spark joy and nostalgia. Recreate your first date, look through old photos, or visit places that hold meaning for you both. These reminders of why you fell in love help keep your connection strong.

Be Playful

Don't take everything so seriously! Bring fun and playfulness into your relationship, whether teasing, playing games, or laughing together. Humor and lightheartedness create an atmosphere of joy and keep the relationship feeling fresh and youthful.

Keep the Romance Alive

Never stop dating your spouse. Keep up romantic gestures like giving compliments, writing love notes, or planning candlelit dinners. Regularly expressing love and appreciation in romantic ways helps prevent complacency and keeps the passion burning.

- **Personal Growth and Individual Interests**

Encourage each other to grow individually as well. Sometimes boredom in a relationship comes from stagnation. When both partners continue to grow—pursuing hobbies, learning, and evolving—it adds energy and excitement that benefits the relationship.

In short, it's about engaging in fun, meaningful activities while balancing personal growth to keep things vibrant and full of life. Keep creating new memories, and boredom will find no space in your marriage or relationship

CHAPTER 3

Unmet Sexual Needs

To keep fulfilling your husband's sexual needs from becoming routine and keep it exciting in a long-term marriage or relationship, here's my advice from experience:

Prioritize Intimacy and Keep It Fresh

Sexual intimacy is an important part of a healthy marriage or relationship, but it can easily become routine or feel like an obligation over time. To keep the sexual connection alive and meaningful, here's what I've learned:

Communicate Openly About Desires

Sexual fulfillment goes beyond just frequency. It's essential to have open, honest conversations about what both of you want and need. Talk about your fantasies, preferences, and any changes in your desires. When you're both comfortable sharing your feelings without judgment, it helps deepen your connection and keeps things exciting.

Change Up the Routine

Avoid falling into a predictable routine by changing things up. Try new experiences, locations, or even different times of day. Being open to trying new things together keeps your physical relationship fresh and stimulating. It also prevents the "same-old" feeling that can sometimes creep in.

Stay Attentive to Emotional Intimacy

Sexual fulfillment is closely tied to emotional intimacy. When you nurture the emotional side of your relationship through affection, meaningful conversation, and shared experiences, it naturally enhances your physical bond. Feeling emotionally close makes physical intimacy more passionate and meaningful.

Prioritize Each Other's Pleasure

Make an effort to understand what brings each of you pleasure. Focus not just on the act itself but on making the experience enjoyable for both partners. This reciprocal attitude ensures both of you feel fulfilled and appreciated in the relationship, reinforcing the connection.

Keep Seduction Alive

Flirt with each other like you did when you first met! Keep the excitement by building anticipation, sending suggestive messages, or surprising him with something unexpected. Playful flirting keeps chemistry alive and breaks up the monotony of everyday life.

Practice Self-Care

Confidence in your own body and sexuality play a huge role in keeping your sexual bond vibrant. Taking care of yourself physically and emotionally not only boosts your self-esteem but also keeps the attraction between you strong.

Make Time for Intimacy

With busy lives, work, and family, it can be easy to let physical intimacy slide down the list of priorities. Make sure you carve out time for intimacy, even if you must schedule it. It sounds less romantic, but prioritizing intimacy shows that you value this aspect of your relationship.

In essence, keeping sexual fulfillment from becoming routine is about variety, communication, and a conscious effort to keep the excitement alive. By staying open, creative, and connected, your physical relationship will continue to feel fulfilling and vibrant, no matter how long you've been together.

For some men, physical intimacy is a primary way they express love or feel connected. When sexual desires or expectations are unmet in a relationship, it may lead them to seek fulfillment elsewhere.

CHAPTER 4

Desire for Novelty

A desire for new experiences, especially sexually, can push some men to cheat. The excitement of something or someone different can be intoxicating, offering a temporary escape from their normal life.

To keep sexual excitement and maintain a strong bond over the years, here's my advice.

Cultivate Playfulness and Emotional Connection to Fuel Sexual Excitement

Maintaining sexual excitement in a long-term marriage or relationship doesn't happen by chance—it requires intention, openness, and a bit of creativity. Here's what I've learned:

Never Stop Flirting

Just because you've been together for a long time doesn't mean the flirtation should stop. Keep the spark alive by flirting like you did when you first started dating. Complement your partner, send flirty texts during the day, or give them that "look" when you're both alone. It keeps the anticipation high and the chemistry fresh.

Be Adventurous and Open-Minded

Keep an adventurous spirit in the bedroom by being open to new experiences. This could mean trying new positions, introducing new elements into your intimacy, or

even role-playing. By exploring new things together, you add an element of excitement and prevent things from becoming predictable.

Build Anticipation

One of the keys to excitement is building anticipation. Don't wait until the moment of intimacy to start connecting. Create a sense of buildup throughout the day or week by teasing each other with subtle touches, loving looks, or suggestive conversations. Anticipation makes the experience more electrifying.

Keep the Romance Alive

Sexual excitement isn't just physical, it's deeply connected to the romance in your relationship. Take time for romantic gestures like candlelit dinners, slow dances, or spontaneous weekends away. Romance strengthens the emotional bond, which enhances passion in your intimate life.

Prioritize Quality Over Quantity

It's not about how often you're intimate, but about how meaningful it is when you are. Focus on creating intimate moments that are fulfilling for both of you, rather than feeling pressured to "keep up" with a certain frequency. Quality, emotionally connected intimacy leaves both partners feeling more satisfied and excited about the next time.

Stay Connected Outside the Bedroom

Strong emotional connection leads to stronger sexual chemistry. Be sure to nurture your emotional bond by talking, laughing, and spending time together doing activities you both enjoy. When you feel connected on an emotional level, physical connection naturally becomes more passionate and exciting.

Be Vulnerable

Vulnerability is the key to deep intimacy. Be open about your desires, needs, and fantasies. Sharing these personal parts of yourself with your partner fosters a deeper bond and keeps the relationship exciting, as it encourages both of you to keep learning about each other even after many years together.

Take Care of Yourself

Self-care is important for keeping the spark alive. When you feel good about yourself—physically and emotionally—you bring that confidence into the relationship, which is incredibly attractive. Take care of your body, mental health, and overall well-being, so you can show up fully in your marriage.

Laugh Together

A great way to maintain excitement is to not take everything too seriously. Laugh together, be playful, and don't be afraid to have fun, even in intimate moments. Humor and lightness help keep the atmosphere relaxed and enjoyable, making your connection feel more spontaneous.

Ultimately, maintaining sexual excitement is about staying curious, continuing to explore one another, and nurturing both your emotional and physical bonds. When you stay engaged, open, and connected, excitement becomes a natural part of your relationship—even after many years together.

CHAPTER 5

Low Self-Esteem

In some cases, cheating is driven by insecurity. A man may seek validation through affairs because it boosts his confidence or makes him feel more desirable or "worthy."

To keep your man's self-esteem high and maintain a strong bond in a long-term marriage or relationship, here's my advice based on experience:

Uplift, Support, and Encourage to Build His Confidence and Deepen the Bond

Men, like anyone else, need affirmation and validation to feel confident in themselves and their role in the relationship. Here's how you can nurture his self-esteem while also strengthening your connection:

Praise His Strengths and Achievements

One of the simplest yet most powerful ways to boost your man's self-esteem is to consistently recognize and celebrate his achievements—both big and small. Whether it's about his career, personal goals, or his role as a partner and father, let him know you see and appreciate his efforts. Hearing praise from the person he loves most will reinforce his sense of worth.

Show Him He's Valued and Needed

Men often find fulfillment in feeling needed and appreciated in the relationship. Show gratitude for the ways he supports you emotionally, physically, or financially. Let him know that his presence, efforts, and contributions matter. Feeling valued and irreplaceable in your life will lift his confidence and strengthen the bond between you.

Offer Emotional Support in Difficult Times

During challenging moments—whether they're work-related, personal, or emotionally his rock. Listen to his concerns without judgment and remind him of his strengths when he's feeling down. By offering unwavering support, you'll show that you believe in him, which helps bolster his self-confidence and solidifies the trust and connection between you.

Compliment Him Sincerely

Compliments aren't just for special occasions. Make it a habit to compliment him regularly, whether it's about his appearance, intelligence, sense of humor, or how well he handles challenges. Genuine, heartfelt compliments make him feel seen and appreciated, boosting both his self-esteem and his love for you.

Encourage His Passions and Growth

Support his personal growth by encouraging him to pursue his passions and hobbies. Whether it's advancing in his career, learning a new skill, or engaging in a favorite activity, he shows interest in what excites him. Your encouragement helps him feel confident in exploring his full potential and keeps the relationship dynamic as you both grow.

Respect His Opinions and Decisions

Respect plays a huge role in building self-esteem. Value his opinions and decisions, even when they differ from your own. Showing that you trust his judgment and respecting his perspective will make him feel respected as a partner, which strengthens both his confidence and your mutual bond.

Show Physical Affection

Physical touch and affection go a long way in making your partner feel loved and desired. Simple gestures like holding hands, hugging, or a spontaneous kiss can reassure him that you're still physically attracted to and connected with him. When he feels desired, his self-esteem naturally rises.

Be His Cheerleader, Not His Critic

There will be times when he makes mistakes or falls short, but instead of focusing on the negatives, focus on how you can encourage and uplift him. Be his cheerleader when he needs motivation and offer constructive feedback in a way that builds him up rather than tearing him down. Positivity in these moments is key to keeping his self-esteem intact.

Create a Safe Space for Vulnerability

Let him know it's okay to be vulnerable around you. Men often feel pressure to appear strong and composed, but providing a space where they can express their fears, insecurities, and emotions without fear of judgment will deepen their emotional bond and boost their self-worth. Knowing he can be himself around you is crucial for maintaining intimacy and trust.

Express Gratitude for His Role as a Partner

Acknowledge the things he does for your relationship, whether it's being a good listener, taking care of household duties, or making sacrifices. Gratitude for his role as a partner shows him that his efforts are noticed and appreciated, reinforcing his sense of value in the relationship.

NOTE: Boosting your man's self-esteem is about affirming his worth, supporting him through highs and lows, and creating an atmosphere where he feels loved, respected, and appreciated. When he feels confident and valued, your emotional bond will naturally grow stronger, creating a lasting and fulfilling partnership.

CHAPTER 6

Opportunity

Sometimes infidelity occurs simply because the opportunity presents itself and the man makes an impulsive decision. The lack of immediate consequences, temptation, and being in an environment conducive to cheating can lead to poor judgment.

To keep your man's self-esteem high and maintain a strong bond in a long-term marriage or relationship, here's my advice based on experience:

Uplift, Support, and Encourage to Build His Confidence and Deepen the Bond

Men, like anyone else, need affirmation and validation to feel confident in themselves and their role in the relationship. Here's how you can nurture his self-esteem while also strengthening your connection:

Praise His Strengths and Achievements

One of the simplest yet most powerful ways to boost your man's self-esteem is to consistently recognize and celebrate his achievements—both big and small. Whether it's about his career, personal goals, or his role as a partner and father, let him know you see and appreciate his efforts. Hearing praise from the person he loves most will reinforce his sense of worth.

Show Him He's Valued and Needed

Men often find fulfillment in feeling needed and appreciated in the relationship. Show gratitude for the ways he supports you emotionally, physically, or financially. Let him know that his presence, efforts, and contributions matter. Feeling valued and irreplaceable in your life will lift his confidence and strengthen the bond between you.

Offer Emotional Support in Difficult Times

During challenging moments—whether they're work-related, personal, or emotionally, be his rock. Listen to his concerns without judgment and remind him of his strengths when he's feeling down. By offering unwavering support, you'll show that you believe in him, which helps bolster his self-confidence and solidifies the trust and connection between you.

Compliment Him Sincerely

Compliments aren't just for special occasions. Make it a habit to compliment him regularly, whether it's about his appearance, intelligence, sense of humor, or how well he handles challenges. Genuine, heartfelt compliments make him feel seen and appreciated, boosting both his self-esteem and his love for you.

Encourage His Passions and Growth

Support his personal growth by encouraging him to pursue his passions and hobbies. Whether it's advancing in his career, learning a new skill, or engaging in a favorite activity, he shows interest in what excites him. Your encouragement helps him feel confident in exploring his full potential and keeps the relationship dynamic as you both grow.

Respect His Opinions and Decisions

Respect plays a huge role in building self-esteem. Value his opinions and decisions, even when they differ from your own. Showing that you trust his judgment and respect his perspective will make him feel respected as a partner, which strengthens both his confidence and your mutual bond.

Show Physical Affection

Physical touch and affection go a long way in making your partner feel loved and desired. Simple gestures like holding hands, hugging, or a spontaneous kiss can reassure him that you're still physically attracted to and connected with him. When he feels desired, his self-esteem naturally rises.

Be His Cheerleader, Not His Critic

There will be times when he makes mistakes or falls short, but instead of focusing on the negatives, focus on how you can encourage and uplift him. Be his cheerleader when he needs motivation and offer constructive feedback in a way that builds him up rather than tearing him down. Positivity in these moments is key to keeping his self-esteem intact.

Create a Safe Space for Vulnerability

Let him know it's okay to be vulnerable around you. Men often feel pressure to appear strong and composed, but providing a space where they can express their fears, insecurities, and emotions without fear of judgment will deepen their emotional bond and boost their self-worth. Knowing he can be himself around you is crucial for maintaining intimacy and trust.

Express Gratitude for His Role as a Partner

Acknowledge the things he does for your relationship, whether it's being a good listener, taking care of household duties, or making sacrifices. Gratitude for his role as a partner shows him that his efforts are noticed and appreciated, reinforcing his sense of value in the relationship.

NOTE: Boosting your man's self-esteem is about affirming his worth, supporting him through highs and lows, and creating an atmosphere where he feels loved, respected, and appreciated. When he feels confident and valued, your emotional bond will naturally grow stronger, creating a lasting and fulfilling partnership.

To nurture mutual respect in a long-term marriage, here's my advice based on experience:

Cultivate Mutual Respect to Strengthen Emotional and Physical Intimacy

Respect is a cornerstone of any strong marriage. It creates an environment where both partners feel valued, understood, and appreciated. Here's how you can maintain respect in your relationship and deepen your bond:

Listen Actively to His Thoughts and Feelings

One of the most powerful ways to show respect is to truly listen when your partner speaks. This means giving him your full attention without interrupting or dismissing his thoughts. When you validate his opinions and emotions, he feels understood and valued. This not only builds respect but also reinforces the emotional intimacy between you.

Appreciate His Perspective, Even When You Disagree

In any relationship, there will be differences of opinion. Instead of dismissing or undermining his viewpoint, take the time to understand where he's coming from. Respect his perspective and acknowledge its validity, even if it's not the same as yours. These fosters open dialogue and mutual understanding, helping both of you grow as individuals while maintaining harmony in the relationship.

Avoid Criticism and Nagging

Respect is easily damaged by constant criticism or nagging. Instead of focusing on what he's doing wrong, highlight what he's doing right, and approach any issues with constructive suggestions rather than complaints. This encourages positive change without making him feel attacked, maintaining respect and trust between you.

Respect His Independence

A strong relationship is built on the foundation of two healthy individuals. Respect his need for space, time to himself, or time with friends. By honoring his independence, you show that you trust and respect him as his person, which strengthens the emotional bond between you.

Celebrate His Strengths

Acknowledging and celebrating his strengths is a powerful way to show respect. Whether it's his work ethic, parenting skills, or how he handles stress, regularly express your admiration for his abilities. This reinforces his self-worth and solidifies mutual respect between you.

• Share Responsibilities and Decisions

Respect in a marriage means valuing each other as equals. Make sure decisions—whether big or small—are made together and that both partners feel heard. Sharing responsibilities, from finances to household chores, shows that you respect his role in the partnership and value his input.

Speak to Him Kindly and With Respect

The way you communicate says a lot about respect in your relationship. Speak to him in a kind, respectful tone, even when discussing difficult topics. Avoid raising your voice, using hurtful language, or speaking condescendingly. How you communicate sets the tone for mutual respect and understanding.

Show Respect for His Time and Efforts

Whether it's about his work or personal life, respect his time and the energy he puts into what matters to him. This includes being mindful of his schedule, understanding when he needs rest or space, and appreciating the effort he puts into providing for and supporting the family.

Support His Personal Growth

Encourage him to pursue his personal interests, career goals, and self-development. Respecting his ambitions and supporting his growth shows that you believe in his potential and value his journey as an individual. When both partners grow and evolve, the relationship thrives.

Apologize and Forgive

Mutual respect also involves humility. If you make a mistake, apologize sincerely. Likewise, be willing to forgive him when he makes an error. Holding grudges or refusing to admit faults can erode respect over time. Acknowledge each other's humanity and offer grace when needed. This strengthens the bond of respect and trust between you.

Note that mutual respect is about recognizing each other's value, honoring each other's individuality, and fostering open communication. When both partners feel respected, the emotional bond grows stronger, creating a solid foundation for a loving, lasting relationship.

Chapter 7

Emotional Insecurity

Men who feel emotionally insecure may cheat to affirm their worth. In some cases, they might believe that having multiple partners elevates their self-image, making them feel more "masculine" or powerful.

To help her husband maintain a strong emotional connection in the marriage or relationship, here's my advice based on experience:

Strengthen Emotional Connection to Keep the Bond Deep and Meaningful

Emotional intimacy is the foundation of a loving marriage. Helping your husband feel emotionally connected strengthens your bond and fosters long-term happiness. Here are ways to nurture and deepen that emotional connection:

Encourage Open, Honest Communication

Make communication a priority in your relationship. Create a safe space where both of you can share your thoughts, feelings, and concerns openly, without fear of judgment. By encouraging him to express himself, you help build trust and emotional closeness. Likewise, share your feelings to foster deeper understanding and connection.

Practice Active Listening

Active listening is key to emotional connection. When he talks, give him your full attention—put away distractions, make eye contact, and listen without interrupting. Show empathy and validate his feelings, even if you don't fully agree. Being a good listener helps him feel understood and supported, which strengthens your bond.

Be Emotionally Available

Life's stresses can sometimes lead to emotional distance in a marriage. Be there for him when he needs emotional support, whether he's going through a tough time at work, dealing with personal struggles, or just having an off day. Offer a shoulder to lean on and remind him that you're his partner through thick and thin.

Show Appreciation for His Efforts

Let him know how much you appreciate him—whether it's for the way he provides for the family, supports you emotionally, or handles everyday challenges. Acknowledging his efforts helps him feel valued and boosts his self-esteem, reinforcing your emotional connection.

Be Affectionate and Supportive

Physical affection and emotional support go hand in hand. Hold his hand, give him hugs, and offer words of encouragement regularly. These small gestures of love and care make him feel cherished, which strengthens the emotional bond between you.

Spend Quality Time Together

Carve out time for just the two of you to connect without distractions. Whether it's going on a date night, taking a walk together, or simply having a meaningful conversation, quality time helps you stay emotionally attuned to each other. This time together reminds him that your relationship is a priority.

Be His Safe Haven

In a world filled with challenges and stress, being his emotional haven is crucial. Let him feel that he can come to you with his fears, insecurities, or problems without being judged or criticized. Offering unconditional love and understanding helps him feel secure in the relationship, knowing he has someone to turn to.

Share in His Joys and Passions

Show interest in his hobbies, passions, and successes. Whether it's a sport he loves, a project at work, or a personal hobby, your involvement or support in the things that matter to him shows that you care about his happiness. Sharing these moments strengthens your emotional connection and helps you grow closer as a couple.

Resolve Conflicts with Compassion

Arguments are inevitable in any marriage, but how you handle them can either strengthen or weaken the emotional bond. Approach conflicts with a desire to understand his perspective and resolve issues with compassion and compromise. Avoid blaming or harsh criticism. Instead, work together to find solutions that bring you closer rather than driving you apart.

Be Vulnerable with Him

Emotional intimacy thrives on vulnerability. Share your fears, dreams, and feelings with him. Being open and vulnerable encourages him to do the same, creating a deeper emotional connection. When both partners feel safe enough to be vulnerable, the relationship becomes a place of mutual understanding and support.

Maintaining a strong emotional connection requires ongoing communication, support, and affection. By being emotionally available, nurturing his needs, and fostering a sense of closeness, you'll help keep your relationship emotionally fulfilling and deeply bonded for the long term.

Chapter 8

Revenge or Retaliation

Some men cheat as a way of "getting even" if they feel betrayed or hurt by their partner, whether it's due to past infidelity or other forms of emotional neglect. This is usually an attempt to hurt their partner in return.

Dealing with a man who is being revengeful or trying to retaliate can be a difficult and emotionally charged situation. If you're a woman in this position, here's some advice on how to handle the situation with care and maintain your emotional well-being while trying to de-escalate the conflict:

Handle a Revengeful Man with Patience, Boundaries, and Clear Communication

When a man is being revengeful, it's coming from a place of hurt, anger, or insecurity. While his behavior is challenging, it's important to approach the situation with emotional intelligence, empathy, and a strategy that protects your well-being. Here's how you can approach this:

Stay Calm and Avoid Reacting Emotionally

One of the most important things you can do is to remain calm. Reacting emotionally or retaliating can escalate the situation. By staying composed, you defuse some of the intensity and show that you're not going to play into the cycle of retaliation. Take deep breaths and give yourself time to think before responding.

Understand the Root Cause

Try to understand what's driving his revengeful behavior. Is it unresolved hurt or anger over something specific? If possible, calmly ask what's bothering him and listen without interrupting or getting defensive. Understanding the root of his actions can sometimes provide insights into how to move forward and resolve the issue peacefully.

Set Firm Boundaries

While it's important to approach the situation with compassion, you also need to protect yourself by setting clear boundaries. Express what behaviors are unacceptable—such as verbal attacks, manipulation, and passive aggressive actions—and that you won't tolerate them. Be firm but respectful when communicating your boundaries.

Don't Feed into the Cycle of Retaliation

If his actions are meant to provoke you, avoid engaging in tit-for-tat behavior. Responding in kind can lead to an escalating cycle of hurt and revenge. Instead, rise above the situation by maintaining your dignity and focusing on constructive solutions. His retaliation will lose power if he sees that you won't engage.

Focus on Open Communication

If the situation allows, have an honest conversation. Use "I" statements to express how his actions are affecting you (e.g., "I feel hurt when you do X") rather than accusing or blaming him. Encourage him to share his perspective so you can both work toward a resolution. Sometimes, open communication can calm feelings of anger or revenge.

De-escalate the Situation

If tensions are high, try to de-escalate the situation by finding common ground. Acknowledge his feelings if they are valid and express a willingness to address the underlying issue. Sometimes just being heard can soften someone's anger. Offer solutions or compromises that could help repair the situation.

Stay Consistent with Your Values

Don't become tempted to respond to revengeful behavior with anger but stay true to your values. Act with integrity, even when the other person is not. Staying grounded in who you are will allow you to handle the situation gracefully and avoid compromising your principles.

• Know When to Walk Away

If the man's behavior becomes toxic or abusive, you have to prioritize your emotional and physical safety. Sometimes, the best option is to walk away from the situation, either temporarily or permanently if the conflict becomes too damaging. It's important to protect your well-being and not remain in a harmful situation.

Seek Outside Support

In some cases, bringing in a neutral third party, such as a counselor or mediator, can help. If the behavior is persistent, professional help can provide guidance and a safe space for both of you to express your feelings and work through the conflict.

Practice Self-Care

Dealing with revengeful behavior can be emotionally draining. Take time to care for yourself—physically, emotionally, and mentally. Surround yourself with supportive friends and family, engage in activities that bring you peace, and allow yourself time to process what's happening. Self-care ensures that you're strong enough to handle the situation.

Don't Take Responsibility for His Actions

While you can work on resolving conflict, remember that his revengeful behavior is his responsibility. You can't control how someone reacts, and you shouldn't take the blame for his actions. Focus on what you can control—your responses, set boundaries, and protecting your peace.

Evaluate the Relationship's Future

Finally, if the pattern of revengeful behavior continues, it's important to assess whether the relationship is healthy. Consistent attempts at retaliation can indicate deeper issues that may not be easily resolved. Consider whether this relationship aligns with your long-term happiness and emotional health.

NOTE: Dealing with a revengeful man requires patience, empathy, and strong boundaries. By staying calm, focusing on communication, and

protecting your mental well-being, you can navigate the situation while maintaining self-respect and peace.

CHAPTER 9

Dissatisfaction with the Relationship

Whether it's an emotional disconnection or general unhappiness, men who feel unsatisfied with the relationship may seek an escape through infidelity, either as a solution or a temporary distraction from their problems.

To help prevent dissatisfaction from taking root in a relationship, here's some advice based on both understanding men's needs and fostering a strong bond:

Prevent Relationship Dissatisfaction by Understanding and Meeting Emotional Needs

The key to maintaining satisfaction lies in nurturing both emotional and physical connection, shared growth, and mutual respect. Here are practical ways to build a fulfilling, balanced relationship:

Communicate Openly and Regularly

Create a habit of open, honest communication. Encourage your partner to share his feelings, concerns, and joys with you, and be willing to listen without judgment. This openness helps both of you stay in tune with each other's evolving needs, preventing misunderstandings and unmet expectations.

Show Appreciation and Acknowledge His Efforts

Consistently showing gratitude for his efforts, whether big or small, reinforces his sense of value in the relationship. Small gestures, words of appreciation, or simply acknowledging his contributions can go a long way in making him feel seen and respected.

Keep the Romance Alive

Over time, couples often fall into a routine that lacks the spark they had at the beginning. Make an effort to keep the romance alive by planning regular date nights, surprising him with small acts of love, or exploring new things together. This helps keep excitement in the relationship and prevents feelings of stagnation.

Be Supportive of His Goals and Dreams

Support his personal and career ambitions and encourage him to grow. By showing genuine interest in his goals and providing encouragement, you contribute to his fulfillment outside the relationship, which translates to more satisfaction within it.

Keep Intimacy a Priority

Physical and emotional intimacy is a cornerstone of satisfaction. Show affection regularly and communicate about your intimate needs and desires. Being receptive and open to his needs in a non-judgmental way fosters closeness and deepens the bond.

Respect His Independence

A healthy relationship balances time together and time apart. Give him the freedom to pursue his hobbies and interests. Respecting his independence allows him to recharge and feel more connected when you are together, creating a healthier dynamism.

Resolve Conflicts Constructively

Dissatisfaction often arises when conflicts are left unresolved or dealt with harshly. Approach disagreements calmly, focus on finding solutions rather than placing blame, and be willing to compromise. Effective conflict resolution builds trust and strengthens the relationship.

Be Open to Growth and Change

People evolve, and so do relationships. Stay open to change and be willing to adapt as both of you grow. Flexibility and understanding as life stages shift— like career changes, family, or personal growth— help prevent dissatisfaction and promote harmony.

Prioritize Emotional Connection

Make emotional closeness a priority by regularly checking in with each other, sharing your feelings, and showing empathy. Creating a safe, supportive environment allows both partners to feel valued and understood, which keeps dissatisfaction at bay.

Take Responsibility for Your Happiness, Too

While meeting his needs is important, remember that your happiness also plays a crucial role. When you are fulfilled and content, it positively impacts the relationship. Taking care of your emotional well-being fosters mutual satisfaction and reduces pressure on him to meet all your needs.

Celebrate Success Together

Whether big or small, celebrate each other's wins. Sharing each other's accomplishments builds a sense of partnership, joy, and pride in the relationship. Celebrating moments together strengthens your bond and keeps your positivity alive.

• Embrace the "Team" Mentality

Approach challenges as a team rather than adversaries. By tackling problems together, both partners feel supported and united. This "we're in this together" mindset reinforces loyalty and deepens connection, helping prevent dissatisfaction.

In summary, preventing dissatisfaction involves creating a strong foundation of appreciation, intimacy, and respect. When both partners feel valued, heard, and supported, the relationship becomes a space of shared joy, fulfillment, and mutual satisfaction.

CHAPTER 10

Immaturity or Lack of Commitment

For some men, infidelity occurs because they haven't fully matured emotionally or aren't ready for the responsibilities that come with a committed relationship. They might cheat because they don't fully grasp the consequences of their actions or feel the weight of their commitment.

When dealing with an immature or noncommittal man, it's important to prioritize your well-being and clarity about what you want in a relationship. Here's advice for navigating this situation while staying true to your needs and boundaries:

Clarify Your Expectations Early On

If you're looking for commitment, make your expectations clear early in the relationship. Express what you want without ultimatums but be honest about your goals. If he's not on the same page, you'll know sooner rather than later.

Observe Actions Over Words

An immature or noncommittal man may talk about wanting a relationship but behave inconsistently. Pay more attention to his actions than his words.

Consistent actions indicate genuine interest and reliability, while inconsistency is often a sign of hesitance or immaturity.

Set Healthy Boundaries

Avoid sacrificing your own needs to keep him around. Set boundaries regarding what you'll accept in the relationship—whether it's exclusivity, quality time, or emotional support. If he repeatedly disregards your boundaries, it's a clear sign he may not be ready for the commitment you want.

Avoid Trying to "Change" Him

Trying to change or "fix" an immature or noncommittal man rarely leads to a fulfilling relationship. Instead, focus on accepting him as he is. If he's not ready or capable of commitment, it's best to acknowledge this and decide whether you can genuinely be content with the dynamic as it stands.

Don't Make Excuses for His Behavior

Sometimes, we rationalize immature or noncommittal behavior because we hope he'll eventually change. Acknowledging reality is crucial; if he's not showing up consistently or respecting your needs, don't downplay it. Recognizing these signs helps you make informed decisions about the relationship.

Avoid Pressuring Him for Commitment

Pressuring or pushing for a commitment can backfire someone who's noncommittal or immature, leading to further distancing. Instead, communicate openly about your desires without demanding commitment. If he's not willing to meet you there, you'll have your answer.

Prioritize Your Growth and Goals

Focus on your own personal growth, career, friendships, and passions outside the relationship. When you invest in your life, you're less likely to settle for a dynamic that isn't fulfilling. A strong sense of self makes it easier to walk away from relationships that don't align with your values.

Be Prepared to Walk Away if Needed

If he isn't showing signs of maturing or committing, be prepared to walk away. Leaving a relationship that doesn't meet your needs is empowering and allows you to open space for someone who shares your vision of commitment. Remember that walking away from the wrong relationship is a step toward finding the right one.

Recognize When It's Time to Move On

If the relationship continually leaves you feeling insecure or unfulfilled, consider whether it's worth the emotional toll. It's better to exit a relationship that doesn't align with your needs than to stay in the hopes of change that may never come.

In essence, dealing with an immature or noncommittal man requires clarity, boundaries, and self-respect. By staying true to what you want and not compromising your needs, you can protect your well-being and leave space for a more fulfilling connection in the future.

CHAPTER 11

Peer Pressure

Believe it or not, social circles can influence cheating behavior. Some men may cheat due to the influence of friends who promote a culture of infidelity, making it seem like it's normal or even expected behavior.

When a man is dealing with pressure, whether from work, family, or personal challenges, it can affect his emotional availability and responsiveness in the relationship. Here's how a woman can support him effectively while maintaining her sense of well-being:

Offer Empathy, Not Solutions

Men often feel pressured to solve problems independently and may become defensive or withdrawn when they feel pressured. Offering empathy without jumping into problem-solving mode can be a powerful way to show support. Sometimes, he just needs someone to listen without judgment or advice.

Create a Safe Space for Communication

Let him know you're there to talk when he's ready, without pushing him to open up immediately. A supportive environment, free of judgment or pressure, can make it easier for him to share his feelings when he's ready.

Encourage Small Breaks and Stress Relief

If you notice he's overwhelmed, suggest low-pressure ways to relax or unwind together, like going for a walk, cooking together, or watching a favorite show. Gentle encouragement can remind him that it's okay to take a breather.

Avoid Taking It Personally

When someone is under stress, they may become distant or irritable. Avoid taking it personally if he's not as responsive or affectionate as usual. Recognizing that this behavior change is due to external pressure rather than a lack of interest helps prevent unnecessary conflict.

Respect His Need for Space

Men often process stress by retreating temporarily. While it may feel difficult, giving him space to sort through his thoughts and emotions can be beneficial. Make it clear you're there for him but allow him room to decompress.

Be Patient with His Process

Pressure can cause people to react differently— some men may become quieter, while others may seem more preoccupied. Let him know that you're patient and that he doesn't have to feel rushed to "fix" things or return to normal immediately.

Encourage Self-Care Without Pushing

Encourage him to practice self-care in a non-pushy way. Whether it's exercise, hobbies, or downtime with friends, remind him that prioritizing his mental and physical health is essential. Sometimes, gentle nudges like "Let's take a break together" are more effective than suggesting he change his routine alone.

Focus on Keeping Things Positive Between You

The relationship can be a source of comfort in stressful times. Try to maintain a positive atmosphere by focusing on light-hearted conversations, humor, or enjoyable shared activities. Being a source of positivity and stability can be incredibly comforting.

Reassure Him of Your Support and Commitment

When people are under pressure, they sometimes worry about whether they're letting their partner down. Reassuring him that you're there for the long haul and that his struggles don't change how you see him; you can reduce his fears and help him feel more secure.

Offering patient, empathetic support when under pressure can strengthen the bond and help him trust that he has a partner who respects his process. This approach not only helps him through his challenges but fosters a deeper connection between both of you.

CHAPTER 12

Thrill of the Chase

The pursuit of a new person can be exhilarating for some men. The "chase" can offer a rush of adrenaline, excitement, and a sense of conquest that is absent from their long-term relationship.

When a man seems to be chasing thrills—whether it's risky behaviors, impulsive decisions, or constant excitement—it often signals that he's seeking an escape or looking to fill a void. Understanding how to handle this healthily can be challenging. Here are some strategies a woman can use to address this situation constructively:

Seek to Understand the Root Cause

Sometimes, thrill-seeking behavior arises from underlying feelings of restlessness, dissatisfaction, or boredom. Try to understand what might be motivating this need for excitement. Approach the topic in a non-judgmental way, asking open questions to help him reflect on what he's feeling.

Communicate Openly About Its Impact

Explain how his thrill-seeking affects you and the relationship. Make it clear that your goal is to understand, not criticize. Communicating your perspective calmly creates a space where he's more likely to open up than become defensive.

Encourage Constructive Outlets for Excitement

Suggest fun, adventurous activities you can do together—like travel, sports, or trying new hobbies. By channeling his need for excitement in positive, shared experiences, you both benefit, and it strengthens your connection.

Avoid Judging or Shaming

It's tempting to express frustration or disapproval, especially if his behavior seems reckless. However, shaming him for his need for excitement can backfire, making him more likely to continue without considering your perspective. Approach the situation with curiosity rather than judgment.

Introduce New Experiences Together

Part of thrill-seeking can stem from a need for novelty. Look for activities you both haven't tried before to add fresh experiences to your relationship. This can help him satisfy that desire for something new and show him that excitement doesn't have to come from outside the relationship.

Help Him Recognize Potential Risks

If his thrill-seeking behavior could lead to harm, such as excessive spending or dangerous activities, have a gentle but honest conversation about the potential consequences. By calmly discussing how these actions may impact his well-being and the relationship, he may start to see the need for moderation.

Support His Personal Growth

Sometimes, thrill-seeking is a way to avoid confronting personal issues or feelings. Encourage him to work on self-reflection, perhaps through journaling or talking to a coach or therapist. Addressing underlying emotions can help him find fulfillment in more balanced, less risky ways.

Encourage Self-Awareness and Balance

Help him explore ways to fulfill his desire for excitement in ways that are healthy and sustainable. Suggest he try activities that offer stimulation without disrupting his stability or the relationship, like intense workouts, creative outlets, or new learning experiences.

Establish Boundaries to Protect the Relationship

If his behavior crosses a line and affects your well-being, it's essential to set boundaries. Let him know how you feel and what's acceptable in the relationship. For example, you might express that reckless spending or impulsive decisions without discussing them with you first are boundaries you aren't comfortable crossing.

Consider Counseling Together

If thrill-seeking is causing significant strain on your relationship, couples counseling can provide tools to manage these issues together. A therapist can help both of you understand underlying needs and guide him in finding balance.

Navigating thrill-seeking behavior requires patience, empathy, and clear communication. By understanding his motivations, encouraging healthy outlets, and fostering shared excitement, you can address his need for novelty while keeping the relationship strong and balanced.

CHAPTER 13

Addiction or Compulsive Behavior

Men who struggle with sex addiction or compulsive behaviors may find themselves cheating repeatedly, unable to control their urges. In these cases, infidelity is driven by deep-seated psychological issues that often require professional help.

When a man is dealing with addiction or compulsive behavior, it requires sensitivity, patience, and often a structured approach to support him while also protecting one's emotional health. Here's how a woman can handle this challenging situation:

Educate Yourself on Addiction and Compulsive Behavior

Understanding addiction and its impact on behavior can help you navigate the situation more effectively. Addiction is a complex issue that often requires professional help. Learning about the cycle of addiction and why certain behaviors persist can increase empathy and help you approach the situation from an informed perspective.

Encourage Professional Help

Addiction recovery often requires guidance from trained professionals. Encourage him to seek counseling, therapy, or addiction treatment programs. Explain that seeking help isn't a sign of weakness but a step toward a healthier, happier life.

Set Healthy Boundaries for Yourself

While offering support is crucial, protecting your emotional and mental well-being is equally important. Establish boundaries to prevent addictive behavior from negatively impacting your life. This could include limits on financial support, communication during certain times, or refusing to enable behavior that feeds the addiction.

Express Support Without Enabling

Show that you're there to support his recovery journey but clarify that you won't enable his harmful behaviors. Enabling includes covering up his actions, making excuses, or providing resources that further fuel the addiction. Instead, focus on providing positive reinforcement for recovery-focused actions.

Practice Patience but Stay Firm on Consequences

Overcoming addiction is a long, often non-linear journey with setbacks. Patience is essential, but so is maintaining a firm stance on consequences if he crosses boundaries. This balance of compassion and accountability can reinforce that while you care, there are limits to what you can accept.

Prioritize Open and Non-Judgmental Communication

Create an environment where he feels safe discussing his struggles without fear of judgment. Instead of criticizing, use "I" statements to express how his actions affect you. For example, "I feel worried when you engage in [behavior] because it impacts our relationship and your well-being."

Seek Support for Yourself

Dealing with a loved one's addiction can be emotionally draining. Support groups like Al-Anon or therapy for partners of those dealing with addiction can provide valuable coping tools and a safe space to share experiences with others who understand.

Encourage Healthy Coping Mechanisms Together

Addiction often develops as a coping mechanism. Encourage healthier outlets, like exercise, hobbies, or mindfulness practices. Participating in these activities together can create positive experiences and help him find alternatives to compulsive behaviors.

Acknowledge His Efforts, Even Small Ones

Positive reinforcement can go a long way. Acknowledge small milestones or improvements, even if they seem minor. Celebrating his progress can motivate him to continue his recovery efforts and feel supported in the journey.

Prepare for Possible Setbacks

Recovery often includes relapses or setbacks. Understanding this can help you stay emotionally prepared and avoid frustration or disappointment if things don't progress smoothly. Setting realistic expectations keeps you resilient and ready to continue offering support without being overwhelmed.

Know When to Step Back for Your Well-Being

If his addiction becomes too damaging or he refuses to seek help, you may need to step back. Recognizing that you cannot change him, no matter how much you care, is important. Sometimes, distance is necessary to protect your own mental and emotional health.

Explore Couples Counseling Together

Addiction impacts relationships deeply. Couples counseling can provide a neutral space to discuss the strain the addiction is causing and create a roadmap for rebuilding trust and connection as he pursues recovery.

Focus on Self-Care and Resilience

Supporting someone through addiction is challenging and can take a toll on your emotional well-being. Prioritize self-care, relaxation, and healthy outlets to keep yourself balanced and resilient, enabling you to be there for him while not losing yourself in the process.

Supporting a partner through addiction is a complex journey that demands compassion, boundaries, and a realistic approach. By staying informed, setting limits, and encouraging recovery-focused behavior, you can provide support while protecting your well-being.

CHAPTER 14

Emotional Avoidance

Some men cheat to avoid confronting the emotional difficulties in their primary relationship. Rather than dealing with the discomfort of open communication, they find temporary comfort elsewhere.

Preventing emotional avoidance in a relationship requires creating an environment where both partners feel safe to express themselves openly. When a woman wants to prevent emotional avoidance, she can encourage vulnerability, set the example for open communication, and create opportunities for meaningful connection. Here are some tips:

Create a Safe Space for Open Expression

Foster a judgment-free environment where your partner feels safe sharing emotions, especially difficult ones. Be patient and show empathy, making it clear that he can express himself without fear of criticism or dismissal. This creates a space where he can be more open over time.

Use Gentle, Non-Confrontational Language

If you sense he's avoiding an emotional topic, bring it up using gentle, non-accusatory language. Phrases like, "I noticed you seemed quiet; is everything okay?" can invite him to share without feeling pressured. Non-confrontational language keeps the conversation light and approachable.

Show Vulnerability First

Sometimes people avoid emotions because they fear being judged or misunderstood. By showing vulnerability yourself, you set a positive example and show that it's okay to express difficult feelings. Opening up about your own emotions—when appropriate—can encourage him to feel comfortable doing the same.

Prioritize Active Listening

When he opens up, even about small things, practice active listening. Show him that his thoughts and feelings matter by giving him your full attention, validating his experience, and responding with empathy. This builds trust and shows that you're truly present.

Encourage Healthy Coping Mechanisms

Sometimes, emotional avoidance is a coping mechanism. Encourage positive outlets, like exercise, hobbies, or mindfulness practices, that can help him process emotions. Offering to do these activities together can make them more appealing and foster a sense of partnership.

Practice Patience and Avoid Forcing Emotional Conversations

If you notice that he's avoiding certain topics, give him time rather than pushing for immediate answers. Gently revisiting conversations when he seems more open can be more effective than pressing him in the moment.

Reinforce Positive Communication with Affirmations

When he opens up, let him know you appreciate his honesty. Acknowledging his openness can make him feel more comfortable sharing. For instance, saying, "I really value that you shared that with me," affirms his willingness to be vulnerable.

Avoid Overreacting to Sensitive Topics

If he shares something that's difficult or surprising, try to respond calmly. Overreactions or intense emotions may cause him to withdraw, worrying about your response to future conversations. Showing that you can handle difficult topics calmly makes him feel safer opening up.

Schedule Quality Time for Bonding

Consistent quality time helps keep emotional intimacy alive. Engage in activities where you both feel comfortable—taking walks, having regular "date nights," or doing something new together. Bonding over shared experiences can naturally lead to deeper conversations and emotional openness.

Respect His Process of Opening Up

Not everyone expresses emotions in the same way or at the same pace. Respect his natural rhythm and avoid pressuring him to talk about every feeling. Being mindful of his pace shows you respect his process and will wait for him to open up in his own time.

Encourage Constructive Expression of Emotions

Suggest different ways he can express his emotions—whether through writing, art, or talking. Not all people find verbal communication easy, so encouraging alternative forms of expression can sometimes make it easier for him to share feelings in a way that feels comfortable.

Consider Therapy for Couples' Communication

If emotional avoidance becomes a recurring challenge, consider suggesting couples counseling. Therapy can provide tools and strategies for open communication and help him work through any barriers he may have with sharing emotions.

By creating a supportive, non-judgmental environment and leading by example, a woman can help her partner feel safe and willing to open up emotionally. Reducing emotional avoidance is often about patience, empathy, and consistent encouragement toward positive communication.

CHAPTER 15

Midlife Crisis

During a midlife crisis, men may experience doubts about their choices, achievements, or even their identity. This often leads to impulsive decisions like cheating in an attempt to reclaim youth or rediscover a lost sense of self.

Supporting a spouse through a mid-life crisis can be challenging, as it often brings intense feelings of confusion, dissatisfaction, and even impulsiveness. Here's how a wife can provide support while maintaining stability in the relationship and protecting her well-being:

• Stay Patient and Compassionate

Understand that a midlife crisis often brings mixed emotions like regret, anxiety, and self-doubt. Practice patience and approach conversations with compassion, reminding him that you're there for support, even if you don't fully understand everything he's going through.

Listen Without Judging or Dismissing His Feelings

Be open to listening actively and avoid judgment. Instead of downplaying his feelings or offering solutions, acknowledge his struggles. Validating his emotions can help him feel understood and reduce his need to seek external validation.

Encourage Open Communication

Creating an environment for honest, open conversations allows him to express his feelings. If he's grappling with uncertainty about his future or questioning his purpose, ask open-ended questions that invite him to explore his feelings further. This can often lead to clarity over time.

Support His Goals and Interests

Sometimes, a midlife crisis may lead to new interests or the desire to revisit old ones. Encourage his passions and pursuits in a supportive way, even if they seem surprising or uncharacteristic. If these activities are positive and safe, they can provide him with a renewed sense of fulfillment and purpose.

Encourage Positive Lifestyle Changes

Midlife crises can trigger the need for physical changes, like improving health and fitness. Support positive lifestyle changes, such as healthy eating or starting a fitness routine together. Focusing on well-being can help him feel energized and centered, offering a healthier outlet for his frustrations.

Suggest Self-Reflection and Self-Improvement

Encourage him to explore self-reflection techniques, journaling, meditation, or therapy. Working with a therapist or counselor can provide an outside perspective, helping him understand his feelings and guiding him to healthier coping mechanisms.

Avoid Taking His Struggles Personally

It's common to feel hurt or confused when a spouse questions his direction or desires. Remember that a midlife crisis is often an internal struggle unrelated to your relationship. Avoid internalizing his actions or words as personal attacks and focus on being a steady presence.

Give Him Space if Needed

If he wants to reflect on his own or spend more time on solo pursuits, try to respect this need for space. Avoid over-checking or pressuring him to talk before he's ready. Giving him room can help him process his feelings more healthily and strengthen your bond.

Encourage Goals and Future Planning

Sometimes, a midlife crisis stems from a feeling of lack of purpose. Encourage him to set new goals for the future, whether that's career changes, travel plans, or learning a new skill. Setting goals can provide a renewed sense of purpose and give him something to look forward to.

Seek Support for Yourself

Supporting a spouse through a midlife crisis can be exhausting and emotionally draining. Don't hesitate to seek help for yourself, whether it's a friend, family member, or therapist. Taking care of your emotional needs ensures you have the resilient to support him without neglecting your well-being.

Consider Counseling for Guidance

If the crisis is straining your relationship, consider couples counseling. A therapist can provide strategies for managing the impact on your relationship and guide both of you toward more constructive ways of coping with his crisis.

Help Him Focus on Gratitude and Positivity

Encouraging gratitude for what's going well can help him shift from a mindset of regret or dissatisfaction. Positives can lead to a more balanced outlook and reduce the tendency to dwell on regrets.

Remind Him of Shared Memories and Strengths in Your Relationship

Revisit positive experiences and shared achievements as a couple to remind him of the good you've built together. This can help him reconnect with the relationship and see it as a source of stability and support rather than something to question.

By being a steady, compassionate presence and encouraging constructive outlets, a wife can support her spouse through a midlife crisis while helping maintain a healthy, balanced relationship. Staying grounded and understanding can ease the transition and allow both partners to emerge stronger.

CHAPTER 16

Escaping from Stress

Work pressure, family responsibilities, or financial issues can create immense stress. Some men cheat as an unhealthy coping mechanism, using the affair to escape or numb the stress they're experiencing in their daily lives.

When a husband is dealing with stress and is trying to escape from it, it can create distance in the relationship and even strain communication. Here's how a wife can be supportive while encouraging healthy ways to manage stress, keeping the relationship close and connected:

Encourage Open Dialogue About His Stressors

Invite him to share what's causing his stress without pressuring him. Gently encourage conversations about what's weighing on him by showing that you're there to listen and support him without judgment or offering immediate solutions. Sometimes, simply having a safe space to express his thoughts helps ease stress.

Show Empathy and Understanding

Let him know that you understand how difficult his stress might feel. Acknowledging his challenges with empathy—without minimizing them—can help him feel validated and understood. Just knowing he's not alone can reduce his urge to escape from the stress and draw him closer to you.

Suggest Healthy Outlets for Relaxation

Encourage healthy forms of stress relief, like exercise, hobbies, or spending time in nature. Sometimes, suggesting activities you can do together—like a walk, a weekend trip, or cooking a meal together—can provide both relaxation and an opportunity for connection.

Give Him Space, But Be Present

While you want to be supportive, it's also important to give him space to process his stress. Let him know you're available whenever he needs to talk or unwind with you, but also respect his need for solitude if that helps him cope. Finding the balance between space and presence can help him feel both supported and respected.

Help Him Focus on Small, Achievable Goals

Stress often feels overwhelming because it seems insurmountable. Encouraging him to focus on small, manageable goals can help him regain a sense of control. Whether it's organizing his workload or tackling household projects, smaller steps can create a sense of accomplishment and reduce stress.

Encourage Self-Care Practices

Remind him of the importance of self-care, whether it's getting enough sleep, eating well, or unwinding in a way that recharges him. Small habits, like a calming evening routine or a favorite weekly activity, can provide an outlet for his stress without the need to "escape" from it.

Suggest Therapy or Counseling as a Constructive Outlet

If his stress is chronic or he seems especially withdrawn, encourage the idea of talking to a therapist or counselor. Therapy offers tools for managing stress constructively. and an outside perspective can help him process his emotions without feeling judged or pressured by family dynamics.

Plan Low-Stress Bonding Activities

Find activities that allow him to de-stress and connect with you without adding to his mental load. A relaxing movie night, a short weekend trip, or even quiet time together over coffee can create positive, low-stress bonding moments. These small breaks help him recharge without feeling overwhelmed.

Reaffirm Your Support and Commitment

Regularly remind him that you're there for him unconditionally. Often, people escape stress because they fear being seen as "less than" when they're struggling. Reaffirming your support builds trust and reassures him that he's not facing his stress alone.

Take Care of Yourself

Supporting someone under stress can take an emotional toll, so make sure you're attending to your needs, too. Finding your balance and maintaining your well-being will help you stay resilient and positive, making it easier to be a supportive partner.

By providing support, patience, and encouragement for healthy coping mechanisms, a wife can help her husband face his stress rather than escape it, strengthening their bond and fostering a healthier relationship.

CHAPTER 17

Feeling Underappreciated

Men who feel undervalued or taken for granted will look for validation outside the relationship. If they feel their efforts or contributions are overlooked, they may seek someone who expresses appreciation for them.

When a husband feels underappreciated, it can lead to resentment, distance, and diminished emotional connection in the relationship. Here are some ways a wife can help him feel valued, respected, and appreciated, fostering a deeper and healthier bond:

Acknowledge His Efforts Regularly

Let him know you notice the things he does, big or small. A simple "thank you" or acknowledging specific actions, like handling a household chore or supporting you in a project, can go a long way. Frequently, sincere appreciation reinforces that his efforts matter to you.

Express Gratitude Through Words and Actions

Besides verbal appreciation, show gratitude in tangible ways that resonate with him. Whether it's cooking his favorite meal, planning a small surprise, or giving him a handwritten note, thoughtful gestures can reinforce how much you appreciate him.

Celebrate His Successes and Achievements

Sometimes, underappreciation stems from feeling overlooked. When he accomplishes something, take time to celebrate it together. Whether it's a promotion, a completed project, or personal growth, acknowledging these wins lets him know his achievements are valued.

Prioritize Quality Time Together

Dedicate time to bond and focus on each other without distractions. Quality time is a powerful way to show that you cherish his company and value your relationship. Plan activities he enjoys and is passionate about to show interest in his world.

Be Supportive of His Goals and Dreams

Even if his ambitions seem different from yours, supporting his goals demonstrates appreciation for his unique path. Ask him about his dreams and plans, and actively encourage him in ways that help him feel you're genuinely interested and on his team.

Show Respect for His Contributions

Appreciation goes beyond compliments—it's also about respecting what he brings to the relationship and family. Whether it's his role as a provider, a caregiver, or a partner, respect his contributions by acknowledging their impact and recognizing the effort he invests in your lives together.

Offer Words of Affirmation

For many people, words of affirmation provide a deep sense of validation. Take a few moments to tell him what you love about him or why you admire him. This can be especially impactful when he's feeling down or unsure, reminding him that he's valued.

Practice Active Listening

When he shares his thoughts, concerns, or feelings, listen, avoid distractions, and try to understand his perspective. Engaged listening makes him feel valued, heard, and understood, reinforcing his appreciation for the relationship.

Take the Initiative to Lighten His Load

If he's feeling overwhelmed or burdened, step in and help without waiting for him to ask. It could mean taking over some chores, running errands, or offering a small break. When he sees you noticing, he's more likely to feel appreciated and supported.

Remind Him of His Strengths and Positives

Sometimes feeling underappreciated stems from self-doubt. Remind him of his strengths, qualities, and the positive impact he has on those around him. Helping him see his worth builds his self-esteem and reminds him that his efforts don't go unnoticed.

Encourage Open Communication About His Needs

Encourage him to share when he's feeling unappreciated or undervalued. Ask open-ended questions like, "How can I support you better?" or "What makes you feel most appreciated?" This shows you're willing to listen and adjust your approach, making him feel valued.

Show Physical Affection to Reinforce Appreciation

Small gestures like a hug, holding hands, or a kiss can communicate appreciation and affection non-verbally. Physical closeness, especially with a simple "I'm grateful for you," reinforces your emotional connection and appreciation.

Avoid Criticizing or Minimizing His Efforts

Criticism can overshadow the positive things he does and make him feel undervalued. If something's bothering you, address it constructively and balance it with acknowledgment of his efforts. Aim for a supportive tone that builds him up rather than bringing him down.

Express Appreciation Publicly (if he's comfortable with it)

Complimenting him in front of family or friends can add an extra layer of appreciation. Just a small compliment or sharing how proud you are of him can help reinforce his value, especially if he appreciates public acknowledgment.

By showing thoughtful appreciation consistently, a wife can remind her spouse of his value in the relationship and foster a stronger, more connected partnership.

CHAPTER 18

Unresolved Past Trauma

Some men cheat because they have unresolved personal issues or trauma, such as abandonment, rejection, or childhood neglect. The affair is a misguided attempt to fill an emotional void they've carried for years.

When a husband is grappling with unresolved trauma, it can affect his emotional health, communication, and the dynamics of the relationship. Here's how a wife can provide support while encouraging healing and growth in a way that maintains her well-being:

Be Patient and Compassionate

Understand that trauma can cause emotional responses and behaviors that might seem confusing or difficult to deal with. Approach him with patience, empathy, and compassion, which helps him feel supported and safe without the pressure of judgment or misunderstanding.

Encourage Open and Honest Communication

Create a safe space for him to talk about his feelings and experiences if he's comfortable doing so. While he might not always want to discuss the trauma directly, letting him know he can share anything without judgment will help him feel less alone and more understood.

Avoid Pushing for Details

While you may want to help him process his trauma, avoid pressing him to share specifics if he's not ready. Trauma often takes time to unpack and pushing him too soon can cause him to retreat emotionally. Respect his boundaries and let him decide when or if to share.

Encourage Professional Help if He's Open to It

Suggesting therapy or counseling can be a constructive approach, as professionals are trained to help people process trauma in a safe and structured environment. Approach this gently, perhaps by framing it to support his well-being and happiness rather than "fixing" an issue.

Educate Yourself About Trauma and Its Effects

Learning about trauma and its impact on behavior, relationships, and mental health can help you understand his responses better. This knowledge can equip you to handle his triggers with sensitivity, making it easier to support him through difficult moments.

Support Self-Care and Healthy Outlets

Encourage healthy coping mechanisms like exercise, journaling, or creative activities, which can help release some of the stress associated with trauma. Supporting him in building self-care habits shows him you care about his well-being and provides an outlet for pent-up emotions.

Respect His Need for Space

There may be times when he needs solitude to process his emotions. Respect his need for space without taking it personally, as this can be an important part of managing the overwhelming emotions that trauma brings. Let him know you're there whenever he's ready to reconnect.

Set Boundaries to Protect Your Own Well-Being

Supporting someone through trauma can be emotionally taxing. Set boundaries to ensure you're also taking care of yourself and not absorbing his struggles as your own. Maintaining your own emotional health will allow you to offer more effective and sustainable support.

Avoid Triggers That May Exacerbate His Trauma

If you're aware of specific triggers that intensify his trauma response, try to be mindful of them. Whether it's avoiding certain topics or limiting exposure to certain environments, showing consideration for his triggers can help create a safer, more understanding environment for healing.

Reinforce Positive Moments and Connections

Trauma can cause someone to become disconnected from the joys of life. Emphasize positive experiences, however small they may be. Whether it's enjoying a shared hobby, spending quality time, or appreciating quiet moments together, these experiences can help ground him and reinforce the strength of your relationship.

Encourage Him to Build a Support Network

A support network of friends, family, or even support groups can be valuable, as it provides different outlets for connection and relief. While you play a supportive role, having others to turn to can broaden his support system and relieve some pressure on the relationship.

Avoid Taking His Reactions Personally

Trauma can sometimes cause irritability, anger, or withdrawal. Remind yourself that his reactions are likely tied to his trauma rather than directed at you. Staying grounded in this understanding can prevent misunderstandings and reduce stress in the relationship.

Practice Self-Care and Seek Your Own Support

Supporting someone with trauma can be challenging, and you need to prioritize your own well-being. Practice self-care, engage in activities that bring you joy, and consider seeking support from friends, family, or even a counselor. A well-supported partner is better able to provide stable, loving support.

Reaffirm Your Commitment and Support

Trauma often causes people to question their self-worth or feel unlovable. Regularly remind him that you're here for him and committed to the relationship, no matter what. This reassurance can counter feelings of unworthiness and create a safe emotional environment that supports healing.

Take it One Step at a Time

Healing from trauma is a gradual process, and it may take time for him to address and work through his experiences fully. Allow the journey to unfold naturally, one step at a time, rather than expecting rapid change. Patience and consistency are essential to fostering a supportive, loving environment.

Supporting a partner through trauma is an act of love, but it's also a commitment to mutual growth and resilience. With compassion, boundaries, and encouragement, you can be a source of strength in his journey while nurturing the bond between you both.

CHAPTER 19

Sexual Dissatisfaction

For some men, cheating is directly related to dissatisfaction with the physical aspects of their current relationship. This can include mismatched libidos, a lack of variety, or simply a lack of sexual chemistry.

When a husband is experiencing sexual dissatisfaction, it's crucial to approach the issue with open communication, empathy, and a commitment to understanding each other's needs. Here are some strategies a wife can consider addressing sexual dissatisfaction while fostering a deeper connection and mutual respect in the relationship:

Initiate an Open and Honest Conversation

Set aside time to discuss sexual satisfaction openly, without judgment or defensiveness. Acknowledge that sexual intimacy is important for both partners' well-being and approach the conversation with curiosity rather than criticism. Use "I" statements (like "I feel..." or "I want to understand...") to create a safe space for both of you to share.

Ask About His Needs and Desires

Encourage him to express what he finds fulfilling or lacking in your intimacy. While it may feel vulnerable, this discussion can lead to a greater understanding of his desires and preferences. Ask open-ended questions like, "What makes you feel most connected?" or "Is there anything new you'd like to try?" to keep the conversation positive and constructive.

Share Your Feelings and Needs

Balance the conversation by sharing your needs and desires too. A mutually satisfying intimate life is about understanding and valuing both partners' preferences. Let him know what brings you pleasure and connection, creating a foundation where both of you can feel more fulfilled.

• Focus on Emotional Intimacy

Sexual satisfaction is often tied to emotional closeness. Strengthening your emotional bond can lead to greater physical connection and satisfaction. Spend quality time together, be affectionate outside of sexual intimacy, and prioritize activities that foster closeness, such as date nights, deep conversations, or shared hobbies.

Consider New Experiences Together

If things feel routine or predictable, try exploring new ways to connect physically. This could be as simple as changing the setting, incorporating a bit of playfulness, or discussing fantasies that interest both of you. Keeping things fresh can reignite the spark and excitement in your intimate life.

Check In on His Stress Levels or External Factors

Sometimes, work, health, or personal stress can interfere with sexual satisfaction. Talk about any stressors he may be facing and consider ways to support each other during challenging times. By acknowledging these factors, you can address underlying issues that may be impacting intimacy.

Work on Physical Health Together

Physical well-being plays a significant role in sexual satisfaction. Discuss ways to incorporate healthy habits together, such as exercise, balanced diets, and good sleep. Sometimes, a few lifestyle adjustments can positively influence sexual energy and mood.

Cultivate a Safe Environment for Vulnerability

When a spouse feels safe to express vulnerabilities without fear of judgment, trust and intimacy deepen. Reassure him that his feelings are valid and that the goal is a satisfying, mutually supportive relationship. This type of openness can help you both feel more connected and willing to explore solutions together.

Explore Professional Help if Needed

If sexual dissatisfaction persists despite open communication, consider seeking the guidance of a couples' therapist or sex therapist. These professionals can provide insight, exercises, and advice tailored to your unique relationship, offering support and helping you work through obstacles constructively.

Regularly Revisit the Topic Gently

Sexual needs can evolve, and it's important to revisit your intimate life periodically to ensure both partners continue to feel fulfilled. Approach the topic from a place of love and curiosity rather than as a problem to fix, allowing space for growth and connection over time.

Be Patient with the Process

Improving sexual satisfaction can be a gradual process, so patience is essential. Emphasize that the journey to a more fulfilling intimate life is one you're taking together, building trust, and strengthening your bond as you work toward greater closeness and connection.

Avoid Blame and Criticism

Rather than framing the issue as someone's fault, treat it as an area for shared growth. A blame-free approach helps both partners feel safe and open, making it easier to understand each other's needs and deepen your physical and emotional connection. By approaching sexual dissatisfaction with understanding, openness, and mutual respect, a wife can support her spouse in feeling valued and connected while also enhancing her own experience within the relationship.

CHAPTER 20

Fear of Intimacy

Ironically, some men cheat to avoid true emotional intimacy. Deep emotional connection can feel overwhelming or vulnerable, so they sabotage the relationship by having affairs to maintain emotional distance.

When a spouse has a fear of intimacy, it can create emotional distance and challenges in the relationship. Approaching this with patience, compassion, and understanding is key. Here are some strategies a wife can consider helping her partner feel safer and more comfortable with closeness:

Create a Safe and Judgment-Free Environment

People with a fear of intimacy often struggle with vulnerability, so creating a safe emotional space is essential. Encourage open conversations without pressuring him to share beyond his comfort level. Being understanding and non-judgmental can foster trust and help him feel safe enough to gradually open up.

Respect His Boundaries and Move at His Pace

It's important to respect his limits when it comes to physical and emotional closeness. Allowing him to take small steps at his own pace helps build comfort. Let him lead in terms of deepening intimacy, reassuring him that you're there whenever he's ready to take the next step.

Express Your Love in Non-Intimidating Ways

Affectionate gestures that aren't overly intense, like holding hands, giving compliments, or sharing laughter, can nurture closeness without overwhelming him. By showing love through everyday interactions, you're fostering a bond in a way that's gentle and reassuring.

Encourage Emotional Intimacy Gradually

Start with non-threatening topics that encourage him to share more of himself. Simple, open-ended questions like "What was your favorite part of the day?" or "What's something you're looking forward to?" can lead to meaningful conversation without feeling intrusive. This can help build emotional closeness without pressure.

Acknowledge and Validate His Feelings

If he expresses anxiety or pulls away, let him know that his feelings are valid. Acknowledging his discomfort without judgment can help him feel understood. By validating his feelings, you can show empathy, making it easier for him to trust and open up over time.

Be Patient and Avoid Pressuring Him

Fear of intimacy often stems from past experiences, which can take time to process. Avoid pressuring him for a deeper connection, as this can push him further away. Reassure him that you're there for him and that you're patient, which can alleviate his anxiety and build trust.

Focus on Building Friendship and Trust

Sometimes shifting the focus from romance to companionship can help foster intimacy more comfortably. Enjoy shared interests, activities, and experiences that help strengthen your connection as friends. A strong foundation of friendship can naturally lead to deeper intimacy over time.

Encourage Professional Support if Needed

For some, fear of intimacy is deeply rooted and may require the help of a therapist. Gently suggest that seeking professional support could be beneficial for his well-being. This may involve individual counseling or couples therapy, which can help both of you understand and address the underlying issues together.

Practice Self-Care and Seek Your Own Support

Supporting a partner with intimacy issues can be emotionally challenging, so it's essential to practice self-care. Consider speaking with a counselor yourself or finding a support network to help you process your feelings and gain insights. Taking care of your needs ensures you're better equipped to support him, too.

Celebrate Small Steps Together

Recognize and celebrate small moments of closeness. Acknowledge each step forward, even if it seems minor. Positive reinforcement can encourage him to continue building intimacy at a comfortable pace, and it reminds both of you that progress is being made.

Communicate Your Needs with Empathy

It's okay to express your own needs in the relationship but frame them in a way that's gentle and understanding. Saying things like, "I love feeling close to you and want us to keep building that" or "I'm here for you, but I also want us to grow closer" shows your commitment without adding pressure.

Addressing fear of intimacy is a gradual process, but with patience, empathy, and understanding, a wife can support her spouse in overcoming these fears. This journey, while challenging, can lead to a deeper connection that strengthens their relationship in meaningful ways.

CHAPTER 21

Fading Physical Attraction

Although it's shallow, some men cheat because they no longer feel physically attracted to their partner. Instead of addressing this issue openly or working to rekindle the spark, they may seek someone who fulfills that physical desire.

If a husband's physical attraction seems to have faded, it can be challenging for both partners. Often, this change reflects shifts in emotional closeness, self-perception, or even life stressors. Here are some thoughtful steps a wife can consider approaching the situation while fostering a deeper connection and appreciation for each other:

Open the Lines of Communication Gently

Start with an open, non-confrontational conversation. Approach the subject by focusing on how you feel rather than making it about him. For example, saying, "I'd love to talk about ways we can feel closer" can encourage honesty and allow both of you to explore the topic without blame or defensiveness.

Foster Emotional Closeness

Often, physical attraction is tied to emotional intimacy. Spend time connecting emotionally by sharing thoughts, dreams, and even worries. Simple gestures like holding hands, planning a surprise, or reminiscing about shared memories can reignite closeness and rekindle physical attraction over time.

Engage in Shared Activities

Trying new activities or revisiting shared interests can add excitement and create moments of enjoyment and discovery together. Whether it's working out, cooking, or taking a weekend trip, spending time doing something different together can build a sense of novelty and connection.

Make Self-Care a Priority

Taking time for self-care can boost confidence and increase your self-perception, which often translates into more positive energy in the relationship. Exercise, mental health practices, or indulging in your interests can contribute to a stronger sense of self, helping you feel attractive and fulfilled, regardless of external feedback.

Focus on Physical Affection without Pressure

Physical closeness doesn't always have to lead to intimacy. Small, affectionate gestures—like holding hands, hugging, or cuddling—create a comfortable and safe space for connection. Consistently showing warmth without pushing for more can help ease any pressure around physical attraction.

Consider Small Changes to Spark Freshness

Sometimes, changing routines or appearances can help bring newness to the relationship. Refreshing your style, rearranging your living space, or planning a surprise date can create a sense of excitement that both partners can enjoy.

Express Appreciation for Him

Share sincere compliments, gratitude, and words of affirmation. When someone feels valued, they are more likely to respond with warmth and attraction. Compliments, whether about his personality, skills, or appearance, can help him feel good about himself and may positively influence his perception of you as well.

Acknowledge External Stressors

Life stressors—like work, health issues, or family responsibilities—can detract from intimacy and attraction. Talk about any pressures you're both experiencing and consider ways to support each other during tough times. Knowing you're both in it together can strengthen your bond and help rebuild the attraction.

Be Patient and Avoid Jumping to Conclusions

Attraction in long-term relationships naturally fluctuates. Avoid taking any lack of physical attraction as a personal flaw or a sign that something is wrong. Give him space to rediscover his feelings without putting additional pressure on the relationship.

Encourage Counseling if Needed

If you notice that distance persists, consider suggesting couples counseling. A professional can help explore underlying causes and give you tools to improve your bond. Addressing these issues with guidance can often lead to a renewed connection and deeper understanding of each other.

By taking these steps, a wife can nurture the bond and rekindle attraction in a gentle, positive way, allowing both partners to feel seen, valued, and connected.

Accepting repeated disrespectful or dismissive behavior in a relationship can have a profound impact on one's mental health and self-worth. Here are a few considerations for recognizing this dynamic and prioritizing personal well-being:

(CHAPTER 22)

BeAware of the Mental and Emotional Impact

Consistently accepting hurtful behavior can lead to feelings of unworthiness, low self-esteem, and increased anxiety. When one's needs are chronically unmet, it can lead to a sense of emotional depletion and self-doubt. Recognizing how this behavior impacts you—mentally and emotionally—is the first step in understanding the need for change.

Recognize the Cycle of Hope and Disappointment

Sometimes, staying in a relationship with repeated patterns of disrespect involves a cycle of hoping things will improve, only to be met with continued disappointment. Understanding that this cycle is unsustainable can help you break free from false hope and instead focus on what is healthy for your well-being.

Realize How Self-Compromise Accumulates Over Time

Compromising your needs to maintain peace or keep a relationship intact can wear down your sense of self. It often leads to resentment, feeling unappreciated, and a loss of confidence. Repeated compromise can distort your perception of what you deserve, leaving you less likely to stand up for yourself over time.

Understand that Self-Respect Sets the Tone for All Relationships

By choosing to put yourself first, you set a powerful example of what respect looks like. When you prioritize self-respect, it sends a message to others that your boundaries and feelings are important. Valuing yourself not only strengthens your mental health but also ensures that future relationships are built on mutual respect.

Reflect on the Long-Term Consequences of Mental Health

Consistently tolerating disrespect can lead to a sense of isolation and even depression. Understanding that mental health must be a priority **means recognizing that a relationship should add value, not take it away.** Feeling valued and safe is essential for your well-being.

Accept That Prioritizing Your Needs Is Not Selfish—It's Essential

Putting yourself first isn't a sign of selfishness; it's a sign of self-respect. It's about protecting your peace, emotional stability, and mental health. By maintaining this standard, you can cultivate relationships where you're truly valued and seen, rather than constantly managing others' needs at the expense of your own.

Seek Support When Needed

Dealing with repeated disrespect can feel isolated, and seeking support from friends, family, or a therapist can provide clarity and strength. Often, an outside perspective can help you recognize the behavior for what it is, and therapy can equip you with tools to set boundaries and regain confidence.

In any relationship, respect and mutual care are foundational. By prioritizing yourself, you foster healthier dynamics and

show yourself the care and kindness that every individual deserves.

Final Thoughts: Infidelity is rarely about one simple reason. Most men who cheat is often driven by a combination of emotional, psychological, and environmental factors. While none of these reasons justify cheating, understanding the underlying motivations can help you address the real issues and foster more honest communication and connection in the relationship.

Copyright Page

Infidelity: 21 Reasons Men Cheat—A Guide for Women Seeking a Lasting, Fulfilling Relationship

Publisher: Felicia Jordan
Editing by: Felicia Jordan
Published in the USA

Closing Thoughts

Love is a journey of passion, discovery, and growth. True love is built not only on moments of romance and connection but on the willingness to understand, adapt, and support each other through life's changes. When two people truly love each other, they share a bond that lets them be fully seen, appreciated, and valued for who they are. Love inspires us to become the best versions of ourselves, not just for our own benefit, but for our partner's as well.

At the heart of love is the ability to learn together. As we move forward in our relationships, challenges arise, and perspectives evolve. These moments offer a chance to grow—individually and as a couple. Real love means sharing dreams and ambitions, cheering each other on, and learning from each other. It's this dedication to shared growth that creates the foundation of a lasting relationship.

Sometimes, love requires us to listen to constructive criticism, an act that calls for vulnerability and trust. When we are open to each other's insights and willing to look at ourselves with honesty, we give love the space to strengthen and mature. Accepting feedback with kindness and understanding allows us to deepen our connection and build a partnership that respects each person's needs.

In the end, love is about choosing to walk alongside each other, to keep growing, and to embrace both the highs and the lows. By doing so, you nurture a love that is true, resilient, and lasting love worth cherishing every day.

115

The Price of Love

They say love's free, yet it drains the soul,
An endless depth, a priceless toll.
No coins exchanged, no fee to pay,
Yet we give ourselves away.

It costs no gold, no silver gleam,
But binds us close, a vivid dream.
No price tag hung, no debt to clear,
Yet love demands all that we hold dear.

We spend our hearts, invest our time,
In whispered words and acts sublime.
A treasure chest, no wealth can chart,
The richest gain—the human heart.

So, here's the truth, though hard to see:

Love's priceless... and it's never free.